MEDJUGORJE
AND
THE MYSTERIES OF
SAINT Joseph

by

a Friend of Medjugorje

SPECIAL STATEMENT

Caritas of Birmingham is not acting on behalf of the Catholic Church or placing its mission under the Church. Its mission is to reach all people of the earth. Its actions are outside of the Church done privately. It is further stated: So as not to take for granted the credibility of the Medjugorje Apparitions, it is stated that the Medjugorje apparitions are not formally approved by the Catholic Church.

Medjugorje Status
December 2, 2021 A.D.

No attempt is intended to pre-empt the Church on the validity of the Medjugorje Apparitions. They are private revelation waiting the Church's final judgment[1]. In the interim, these private revelations **are** allowed by, and for, the faithful to have devotion to and to be spread legally by the Church. Devotion and the propagation of private revelations can be forbidden only **if** the private revelation is condemned because of anything it contains which contravenes faith and morals according to AAS 58 (1966) 1186 Congregation for the Doctrine of the Faith. Medjugorje has not been condemned nor found to have anything against faith or morals, therefore it is in the grace of the Church to be followed by the faithful. By the rite of Baptism one is commissioned and given the authority to evangelize. *"By Baptism they share in the priesthood of Christ, in His prophetic and royal mission."*[2] One does not need approval to promote or to have devotions to private revelations or to spread them when in conformity to AAS 58 (1966) 1186, as the call to evangelize is given when baptized. These apparitions have not been approved formally by the Church. Caritas of Birmingham, the Community of Caritas and all associated with it, realize and accept that the final authority regarding the Queen of Peace, Medjugorje and happenings related to the apparitions, rests with the Holy See in Rome. We at Caritas, willingly submit to that judgment. While having an amiable relationship with the Diocese of Birmingham and a friendly relationship with its bishop, Caritas of Birmingham as a lay mission is not officially connected to the Diocese of Birmingham, Alabama, just as is the Knights of Columbus [3] The Diocese of Birmingham's official position on Caritas is neutral and holds us as Catholics in good standing.

1. The Church does not have to approve the apparitions. The Church can do as She did with the apparitions of Rue du Bac in Paris and the Miraculous Medal. The Church never approved these apparitions. She gave way to the people's widespread acceptance of the Miraculous Medal and thereby the Apparitions to St. Catherine. *Sensus Fidelium* (Latin, meaning "The Sense of the Faithful"), regarding Medjugorje, is that the "sense" of the people says that "Mary is here (Medjugorje)."
2. Catechism of the Catholic Church Second Edition.
3. The Knights of Columbus also are not officially under the Church, yet they are very Catholic. The Knights of Columbus was founded as a lay organization in 1882, with the basic Catholic beliefs. Each local council appeals to the local Ordinary to be the Chaplain. The Knights of Columbus is still a lay organization, and operates with its own autonomy.

Published with permission from SJP Lic. COB.

© 2021, S.J.P. Lic. C.O.B.

ISBN: 978-1-878909-49-7

Printed and bound in the United States of America.

©SJP International Copyright. All rights reserved including international rights. No part of this book may be reproduced or transmitted in any form or by any means, electronic or mechanical, including photocopying, recording, or by any information storage or retrieval system, without permission in writing from Caritas who is licensed to use the material. Caritas of Birmingham, 100 Our Lady Queen of Peace Drive, Sterrett, Alabama 35147 USA. None of the mailing lists of Caritas or its entities, including electronic mailing lists, etc., are for sale, nor is permission given to use them in anyway, by anyone. There are no exceptions. All civil, criminal and interstate violations of law apply.

For additional copies, contact your local bookstore or call
Caritas of Birmingham at 205-672-2000 USA.

MEDJUGORJE
AND
THE MYSTERIES OF
SAINT Joseph

by

a Friend of Medjugorje

Published with permission from SJP by
CARITAS OF BIRMINGHAM
STERRETT, ALABAMA 35147 USA

About the Witness

Many who will read these books have been following the writings of a Friend of Medjugorje for years. His original and unique insights into the important events of our day have won credence in hundreds of thousands of hearts around the world, with those affecting others, thereby, touching into the millions. His moral courage in the face of so many leaders caving in to the pressures of a politically correct world is not only refreshing, but, according to tens of thousands of written testimonies over 32 years, has helped to strengthen deeply those who desire to live the fullness of their Christian faith. His insights have repeatedly proven prophetic, having their source in the apparitions of the Virgin Mary in Medjugorje. Deeply and personally influenced by the events surrounding Medjugorje, he gave himself to the prayerful application of the words of the Virgin Mary into his life. He has spoken all over the world on Our Lady's messages and how to put them into everyday life. He came to understand that Our Lady was sent by God to speak to mankind in this time because the dangers man is facing are on a scale unlike any the world has ever known since Noah and the flood. He is not an author. He is a witness of what Our Lady has shown him to testify to—first, by his life—secondly, through the written word. He is not one looking in from the outside regarding Medjugorje, but one who is close to the events—many times, right in the middle of the events about which he has written.

Originally writing to only a few individuals in 1987, readership has grown well into the millions in the United States and in over 130 foreign countries, who follow the spiritual insights and direction given through these writings.

When asked why he signs only as "a Friend of Medjugorje," he stated:

"I have never had an ambition or desire to write. I do so only because God has shown me, through prayer, that He desires this of me. So from the beginning, when I was writing to only a few people, I prayed to God and promised I would not sign anything; that the writings would have to carry themselves and not

be built on a personality. I prayed that if it was God's desire for these writings to be inspired and known, then He could do it by His Will and grace and that my will be abandoned to it.

"The Father has made these writings known and continues to spread them to the ends of the earth. These were Our Lord's last words before ascending: **'Be a witness to the ends of the earth.'** *These writings give testimony to that desire of Our Lord, to be a witness with one's life. It is not important to be known. It is important to do God's Will."*

For those who require "ownership" of these writings by the 'witness' in seeing his name printed on this work in order to give it more credibility, we, Caritas of Birmingham and the Community of Caritas, state that we cannot reconcile the fact that these writings are producing hundreds of thousands of conversions, and will easily be into the millions, through God's grace. His writings are requested worldwide from every corner of the earth. His witness and testimony, therefore, will not take credit for a work that, by proof of the impact these writings have to lead hearts to conversion, has been Spirit–inspired, with numbers increasing yearly, sweeping as a wave across the ocean. Indeed, in this case, crossing every ocean of the earth. Our Lady gave this Witness a direct message, through the Medjugorje visionary, Marija, and part of what Our Lady said to him was to **"...witness not with words but through humility..."** (Oct. 6, 1986) It is for this reason that he wishes to remain simply, "A Friend of Medjugorje."

In order to silence the voice of this witness, darkness has continually spewed out slanders to prevent souls from reading his convicting and life-changing writings. For if these writings were not so, darkness would ignore them or even lead people to them. But Jesus promised persecution to all those who follow Him, and the same will be to those who follow His Mother. *"If they persecuted me, they will also persecute you."* John 15:20

As a witness in real-time of Our Lady's time on earth, his witness and writings will continue to speak—voicing Our Lady's Way to hundreds of millions not yet born—in the centuries to come.

— Caritas of Birmingham

Medjugorje
The Story in Brief

A VILLAGE SEES THE LIGHT is the title of a story which "Reader's Digest" published in February 1986. It was the first major news on a mass public scale that told of the Virgin Mary visiting the tiny village of Medjugorje, Bosnia-Hercegovina. At that time this village was populated by 400 families.

It was June 24, 1981, the Feast of John the Baptist, the proclaimer of the coming Messiah. In the evening, around 5:00 p.m., the Virgin Mary appeared to two young people, Mirjana Dragičević* and Ivanka Ivanković*. Around 6:40 p.m. the same day, Mirjana and Ivanka, along with four more young people, Milka Pavlović*, the little sister of Marija, Ivan Ivanković, Vicka Ivanković*, and Ivan Dragičević saw the Virgin Mary. The next day, June 25, 1981, along with Mirjana, Ivanka, Vicka and Ivan Dragičević, Marija Pavlović* and Jakov Čolo also saw the Virgin Mary, bringing the total to six visionaries. Milka Pavlović* and Ivan Ivanković only saw Our Lady once, on that first day. These six have become known as and remain "the visionaries."

These visionaries are not related to one another. Three of the six visionaries no longer see Our Lady on a

* Names at the time of the apparitions, they are now married with last names changed.

daily basis. As of December 2021, the Virgin is still appearing everyday to the remaining three visionaries; that's well over 17,314 apparitions. This count is each day for all the visionaries together in the apparitions. The visionaries have been separated for more years than together, which means the number is minimum 30 years × 3 visionaries who still see Our Lady daily being separated during apparition time.

The supernatural event has survived all efforts of the Communists to put a stop to it, many scientific studies, and even the condemnation by the local bishop; yet, the apparitions have survived, giving strong evidence that this is from God because nothing and no one has been able to stop it. For over 40 years, the apparitions have proved themselves over and over and now credibility is so favorable around the world that the burden of proof that this is authentic has shifted from those who believe to the burden of proof that it is not happening by those opposed to it. Those against the apparitions are being crushed by the fruits of Medjugorje — millions and millions of conversions which are so powerful that they are changing and will continue to change the whole face of the earth.

See **mej.com** for more information.
or **Medjugorje.com**

Acknowledgement

God alone deserves the credit for the publication of this book. It is from Him that the messages are allowed to be given through Our Lady to all of mankind. He alone deserves the praise and honor.

Table of Contents

II	ABOUT THE WITNESS
VI	MEDJUGORJE THE STORY IN BRIEF
X	PREFACE

CHAPTER ONE
1   THE SIGNIFICANCE OF THE NUMBER 18

CHAPTER TWO
9   WHAT IS THE SIGNIFICANCE OF THE ACTUAL DATE: MARCH 18TH? NOT ONLY THE 10 SECRETS BUT ARE THERE SECRETS ABOUT ST. JOSEPH TO BE REVEALED?

CHAPTER THREE
19   WHY JOSEPH? WHY NOW?

CHAPTER FOUR
27   APPARITIONS OF ST. JOSEPH THROUGH TIME

CHAPTER FIVE
63   A MYSTERY OF ST. JOSEPH REVEALED

CHAPTER SIX
77   JOHN THE BAPTIST: THE LAST PRIEST

CHAPTER SEVEN
87   ST. JOSEPH: THE LAST KING

APPENDIX
99   PARALLELING HEAVEN'S ACTIONS, THE POPES FOLLOW SUIT

PREFACE

During the research phase of writing the soon to be released book, <u>The Ten Secrets of Medjugorje: Where We Stand</u>, a Friend of Medjugorje discovered many fascinating facts that led him down many pathways of discovery. While some of these discoveries were relevant to the Ten Secrets, some of the topics needed to be expanded in a separate publication. That was the case in what was discovered about St. Joseph. Our Lady of Medjugorje has not said anything that has been made public about St. Joseph through Her visionaries. However, a Friend of Medjugorje has followed signs and clues that Our Lady gave through Her actions and messages that point strongly to the probability that St. Joseph has a part to play in the fulfillment of Our Lady's plans for the salvation of the world. In <u>Medjugorje and the Mysteries of Saint Joseph</u>, a Friend of Medjugorje, takes the reader on a path following each clue that leads one to surprising places.

What was the first clue that a Friend of Medjugorje started from? The date Our Lady gave to Medjugorje visionary, Mirjana, as a promise that She would appear to her on that day every year for the rest of her life. What was the date? March 18th. How does it relate to St. Joseph? You will discover the answers through the unfolding of these pages.

—Caritas of Birmingham

"This man, Joseph, is going to come into our future even more, through Medjugorje, because he is the third part of the Holy Family, a small reflection of a trinity, who will remind the world how to bring holiness back into the family." [1]

Friend of Medjugorje
"Joseph's Advice to Jesus"
©2019

CHAPTER ONE

The Significance of the Number 18

The number 18 is a clue that Our Lady has given to us. Medjugorje visionary, Mirjana, has revealed that there will be some great event that will take place on a future March 18th. She relayed that when the event happens, everyone will understand why March 18th was chosen. That is a very big clue. It gives us a place to start in hunting for significance and possible indications of what March 18th could be connected to. Does the number 18 have significance in other events in the past? Looking at other Marian apparitions there is a surprising correlation with the number 18. In the most significant apparitions, the number 18 comes up over and over again.

- Paris, France — **18**30

St. Catherine Laboure first saw Our Lady in Rue de Bac in Paris on July <u>18</u>, <u>18</u>30.

- Lourdes, France — **<u>18</u>**58

    Our Lady appeared to St. Bernadette **<u>18</u>** times, beginning on February 11, **<u>18</u>**58.

    On February **<u>18</u>**, **<u>18</u>**58 Our Lady spoke to Bernadette for the first time.

    On July 16, **<u>18</u>**58, the **<u>18</u>**th and final apparition took place on the Feast of Our Lady of Mt. Carmel.

- Garabandal, Spain — 1961-1965

    The apparitions of Our Lady in Garabandal have not yet been approved and it is not our mission to promote them, however, there are many similarities between Garabandal and Medjugorje that give some credence to the authenticity of Garabandal. In particular, for this discussion, their connection to the number **18**.

In the apparitions of Garabandal, the first and last messages for the world were given on October **18**, 1961 and June **18**, 1965.

The first apparition of St. Michael was on June **18**, 1961, and the Miracle of the Host took place on July **18**, 1962.

From the above, we can see that the number 18 wasn't just randomly selected from Heaven, but that it connects to other apparitions of Our Lady from the past. This was an encouragement to continue to look for other clues and it didn't take long before another connection was found.

The Number 18 in the Hebrew Language

The Hebrew language is the language God spoke. It is the language that all the prophets of the Old Testament spoke to deliver God's messages to His people. Hebrew is the national language of the Jewish people and is virtually unchanged throughout thousands of years. Our Lady is Jewish. She was raised under the Jewish laws, lived the culture and traditions of Judaism, and was chosen by God to bring the Jewish Messiah into the world. Becoming a Christian wasn't a denunciation of the Jewish faith, but the fulfillment of the Jewish faith. The Hebrew language is older than all modern languages. Its letters are pictures and each Hebrew letter, it is said, contains a message from God. Hebrew letters also represent numbers.

*"The values of the **letters** in a word or phrase can be added up and converted to a number. Words and phrases with the same value can then be compared, revealing a hidden relationship between them that can teach some deeper meaning or **message**."*[2]

In following down this path, a major clue was discovered concerning the number 18.

Chai (חי) is the **Hebrew** word for **LIFE**. The word, consists of two **Hebrew letters** —

Chet (ח) which has the numerical value of **8** and

Yud (י) which has the numerical value of **10.**

Add the two numbers together: **8 + 10** gives the **numerical value of 18.**

So, the number 18, in the Hebrew language, the language of God, has great meaning. It literally means **LIFE**.

But how does this connect to Our Lady and Medjugorje? Our Lady gave Medjugorje visionary, Vicka, the specific task of writing down everything She (Our Lady) told her (Vicka) pertaining to Our Lady's life. Vicka filled three notebooks of stories regarding Our Lady's life, never before revealed. When Vicka was asked what the title of the book will be, Vicka answered that it is simply called, **"LIFE."** So, what can be said so far:

- The number **18** has significance in other Marian apparitions.

- Through Mirjana, we know some significant event will take place on a future **March 18th**.

- In the Hebrew language, the number **18** means **LIFE**.

- Vicka was given the title, **LIFE**, for Our Lady's life story.

From the above, we can deduce that the number **18** is not only significant, but is connected to Our Lady's own life in some way. She certainly was taught the meaning of the Hebrew alphabet and the mysteries contained within it early in Her life on earth. Choosing to name the story of Her life, as **"LIFE,"** points also to a deeper mystery. Was there more to discover? There is always more to discover when dealing with Our Lady.

"We wonder why the Gospel makes so little mention of St. Joseph. But did it not say everything when it taught us that he was the husband of Mary?"

Blessed William Joseph Chaminade

CHAPTER TWO

What is the Significance of the Actual Date: March 18th?
Not Only the Ten Secrets, But Are There Secrets About St. Joseph to be Revealed?

Knowing something of great importance is going to happen on a future March 18th, the obvious question to ask would be if March 18th already is a significant date, or connected to a significant event that would help to shed light on what the future event Our Lady has foretold could be.

Looking first at the month of March, there is a great feast day of Our Lady that lands on March 25th each year, which is the Feast of the Annunciation. God sent His messenger angel, Gabriel, to Our Lady's home with the request that She would become the Mother of the Savior. Our Lady gives

Her Fiat, Her yes, and the time of man's redemption entered real time. The Church set this feast on March 25th because it is nine months before Christmas Day, December 25th, the Birth of Jesus Christ. But, at the same time, March is also the time of Lent, preparation for the commemoration of the Death and Resurrection of Our Lord. So, in this particular month, unique to all other months, the whole life of Jesus Christ, from Conception to Death, which Our Lady was intimately connected to is brought full circle. There's that word again: **LIFE**.

But what does that have to do with March 18th? The main significance to March 18th is that it is connected to March 19th, which is the Feast of St. Joseph. St. Joseph has more than one feast day. May 1st is also a day designated to honor St. Joseph the Worker. But March 19th is the principal feast day to honor Joseph as the husband of the Virgin Mary and the "foster" father of Jesus Christ, his place in the Holy Family. You might say, well that day is March 19th, which doesn't connect to March 18th. Yet, it does.

In the Jewish faith, a day starts in the evening, at sundown and ends the following sundown, so a day always moves from dark to Light, rather than most of the world that live their days from morning to evening, dawn to dusk, Light to dark. Why? Because of what Genesis 1:1–3 says:

> ***"In the beginning, when God created the heavens and the earth, the earth was a formless wasteland, and darkness covered the abyss, while a mighty wind swept over the waters. Then God said, 'Let there be light,' and there was light. God saw how good the light was. God then separated the light from the darkness he called 'night.' <u>Thus evening came, and morning followed--the first day.</u>"*** Gen. 1:1-3

This is a revelation to most Christians. Yet, in the Christian faith, you also can see this pattern. Liturgically, the Christmas celebration begins on Christmas Eve. The Eve of All Hallows (Halloween) leads into the celebration on All Saints Day. New Year's Eve brings the dawn of the Feast of Mary, the Mother of God. From the Good Friday and Holy Saturday evening vigils arises Easter Morning. And amazingly, in pondering the actions of Our Lady of Medjugorje over the past 40 years, the vigils of feast days also hold great significance.

In 1981, Our Lady first appeared on June 24th on the Feast of St. John the Baptist. Yet, when Our Lady was asked when She wanted Her anniversary celebrated, She answered saying:

February 2, 1982

"I would prefer that it take place June 25th. The faithful have come for the first time on that day, on the hill."

Yet, despite Our Lady naming June 25th the feast of the anniversary of Her apparitions, every year the celebration begins on June 24th, the vigil of the feast day. The time of Our Lady's apparitions in Medjugorje over the past 40 years is also mysterious. On June 24, 1981, She appeared at 6:40 PM, at sundown. Is this not a sign that Our Lady has come to lead the world out of the darkness into the Light? Our Lady is dawning a new day for the Church and for man through this time given to Her by God in Her apparitions.

There are other circumstances in which Our Lady emphasized the vigil of an event. For example, Marija has come to Caritas of Birmingham in Alabama for the Consecration of the United States of America, July 3–4, in the years 2008, 2009, 2012 and 2013. In each of those years, Our Lady honored both the vigil, July 3rd, and the actual feast day of July 4th with special apparitions and has even given a message on the night of the vigil on a couple of occasions, rather than on the actual 4th of July feast day.

These are only a few clues to point to March 18th as possibly being significant because it is the vigil of the Feast of St. Joseph. But consider this in the larger context of what we are discovering. How is it that the vigil and feast of St. Joseph, March 18 and 19 aligns so perfectly to the meaning of the number 18, which is LIFE, and with the story of Our Lady's LIFE, as revealed to Vicka. Add to that the close proximity of March 18 and 19 to the Feast of the Annunciation, which begins the LIFE of Jesus, in the Virgin's womb. One can see that Joseph's presence is being made more known within the circle of the Holy Family and not as a minor character, but one with great significance.

What this suggests is that in the story of Our Lady's life as revealed to Vicka, we may learn not just about Our Lady's life, but also about St. Joseph—the man he was, Our Lady's marriage to him, Joseph as father to Jesus, their life together as a family, their relationships, etc. Church tradition tells us that Mary was 15 or 16 years old at the time of the Annunciation. That St. Joseph died near the time that Jesus was going to begin His public ministry. That Our Lady's Assumption into Heaven took place before She had turned 60 years old. Even if those are approximate years, it still can be said that when considering Her entire LIFE, Our Lady shared at least half of Her life with St. Joseph. Therefore, there is much to learn of those hidden years of the Holy Family. What would Our Lady want to teach us about St. Joseph? In <u>The Poem of</u>

the Man-God,* by Maria Valtorta, Volume I, Our Lady says this about Joseph:

> "[Joseph] should be appointed protector not only of dying people, of married couples, of workmen, but also of those consecrated to God. Who, of all the people in the world consecrated to the service of God, has consecrated himself as he did, to the service of his God, accepting everything, foregoing everything, bearing everything, fulfilling everything with quickness, with a cheerful mind [and] a constant humor..."³

---

* Medjugorje visionary, Marija, went before Our Lady on behalf of a seminarian and asked the question: *"Was it okay to read the book The Poem of the Man-God?"* Marija relayed that Our Lady affirmed it was okay by answering: **"One can read them."**

Because a storm of opposition erupted as a result of the writings of Maria Valtorta's growing popularity, Caritas of Birmingham, Cardinal Ratzinger, and Pope John Paul II are recorded in Church history as a result of a verdict rendered concerning The Poem of the Man-God.

The historic Church ruling cleared the way for the faithful to read the volumes. The Church only required they not be declared supernatural. This is always the way the Church works. Time gave the historic decision to Caritas and time will further clarify. What is important now is the Church's approval for the faithful to read them, and that The Poem of the Man-God can be read, correlates to Our Lady's words, **"One can read them."**

Did you read that? Of all the saints who have ever lived, no one has ever consecrated themselves to the service of God as fully as Joseph did. Our Lady ends this above quoted passage from The Poem of the Man-God,* saying:

"...There is no one like him."[4]

What will we learn about St. Joseph? Is Our Lady preparing to give the world a window into the life of St. Joseph as never before?

---

* See footnote on previous page

"In St. Joseph the Old Testament finds its fitting close. He brought the noble line of patriarchs and prophets to its promised fulfillment. What the divine goodness had offered as a promise to them, he held in his arms."

St. Bernardine of Siena

CHAPTER THREE

Why Joseph? Why Now?

Let us turn to the only message in which Our Lady speaks of Fatima:

August 25, 1991

> **"...I invite you to renunciation for nine days so that with your help everything I wanted to realize through the secrets I began in Fatima may be fulfilled..."**

Fatima visionary, Sr. Lucia, revealed to Cardinal Carlo Caffarra in 1984:

> *"Father, a time will come when the decisive battle between the Kingdom of Christ and satan will be over marriage and the family."*[5]

Our Lady of Medjugorje told the visionaries that once the Secrets take place, it will no longer be necessary for Our Lady to return to the earth through apparitions where one can see, touch, hear and speak to Her. Why? Because everything necessary will have been given to man for his salvation until the end of time once God's plans through Medjugorje are fulfilled.

What does this mean and where does St. Joseph fit into the picture? After Jesus' Death and Resurrection, it took many centuries to spread and define the faith of Jesus Christ in His newborn Church. Mary was kept in the shadows for fear that those coming out of pagan lives would turn Her into a goddess. They, therefore, were cautious to give Mary too much attention. With the Protestant Reformation, Mary was left out altogether, and relegated to only a brief appearance at Christmastime. Though Catholics have always been taught to revere and love Mary, with greater emphasis on

Ecumenism over the past century, many theologians insisted on keeping Mary in the shadows.

God would not allow this, however. He raised up apostles of Our Lady throughout time, such as St. Louis de Montfort, St. Maximillian Kolbe and Pope St. John Paul II to reveal the depth of Our Lady's love for mankind and for the Church. But more than that, He sent Our Lady Herself, throughout history. In every appearance, Our Lady revealed something more of Herself, and the special position She holds in the plan of salvation. As I have said for decades, Medjugorje is the fulfillment of all Her Marian Apparitions.

Our Lady's apparitions in Paris, France; Lourdes, France; Guadalupe, Mexico; Fatima, Portugal; Knock, Ireland; Medjugorje, Bosnia-Herzegovina and even Her apparitions at Caritas near Birmingham, Alabama, serve to make Our Lady known and have created a following that has grown through time, passing from generation to generation. This spiritual movement birthed from the apparitions of the Virgin Mary is the most powerful and successful evangelization movement the Church has experienced in reaching and converting souls. Nothing can come close to what the Virgin Mary can do in bringing hearts back to the Church and back to Her Son. It is why God sent Her.

Enter now St. Joseph. For the importance St. Joseph holds in the life of Jesus Christ, he is the most neglected saint. Take for instance St. Joseph's popularity compared to St. Patrick's, whose feast day falls two days before St. Joseph's. The celebration of the latter far exceeds the tribute given to St. Joseph around the world. Yet, if you look in the Daily Prayers of the faithful, St. Joseph is given the full treatment of a highly exalted saint, including the Vigil prayers, antiphons, etc., while St. Patrick gets only a prayer and two antiphons for his feast. This is not to downplay St. Patrick, but to make us question, why St. Joseph isn't treated with higher honor and regard, though he, for 30 years, singularly provided for, protected, and cared for God, Himself, in the form of Man, and the Virgin Mary who brought the Messiah into the world.

If this seems unbalanced to us, how does it appear from Heaven's point of view? There can only be one reason why St. Joseph has been literally, disregarded by so many in the Church for so long. It has been by God's design. Consider this prophecy regarding St. Joseph from the 16th Century:

> Isadore of Isolanis, a pious Dominican of the 16th century, prophesied that *"the sound of victory"* will be heard in the Church Militant *"when the faithful recognize the sanctity of St. Joseph."* He continues: *"The Lord will let His light shine, He will lift the veil, and great men will search out the interior gifts of God that are hidden in St. Joseph; they will find in him a priceless treasure, the like of which they had never found in other saints of the Old Testa-*

ment. *We are inclined to believe that towards the end of time, God will overwhelm St. Joseph with glorious honor. If in the past ages during the storms of persecution, these honors could not be shown to St. Joseph, we must conclude that* **they have been reserved for later times.** **At some future time, the feast of St. Joseph will be celebrated as one of the greatest feasts.** *The Vicar of Christ, inspired by the Holy Spirit, will order this feast to be celebrated in the Universal Church."* [6]

Could this be what March 18th is about, at least in part? As Our Lady appeared on the horizon long before She came onto the center of the world's stage, can we look back and say the same is true of Joseph? We have more than prophecy. We have Heaven's action to show that God's plan for the Salvation of the World as delivered through the apparitions of Our Lady through Medjugorje may just include taking St. Joseph from off of the sidelines, where he has stood for the past 2,000 years, and putting him in the game as a star player. And it is none other than the Virgin Mary who is calling him out on the stage to take his place beside Her.

"We cannot help but feel how Our Lady is pleased by this honor due to the humblest of God's servants, Joseph, who in his hiddenness, led Our Lady and Jesus in this worldly life, yet, also, led by them, now revealing Fatherhood to the world." [7]

Friend of Medjugorje
"Father, Revelations"
medjugorje.com[7]

CHAPTER FOUR

Apparitions of St. Joseph Through Time

It is not until the 1800s (the number 18 again!), that appearances of St. Joseph begin to be noticed. By contrast, Our Lady's appearances began centuries before, but did also accelerate in the 1800s. It should be noted that several of the apparitions with Our Lady in the 1800s included St. Joseph. Another "sign" from Heaven?

What follows is not a comprehensive look at all apparitions with St. Joseph. Rather the focus is on those apparitions which support the supposition that the plan of salvation, through Our Lady of Medjugorje, is leading to a time in which St. Joseph will come out of the shadows into the fullness of the authority given to him when he was chosen to become the father-guardian of Jesus Christ and spouse to the Most Holy Virgin Mary. Each of the apparitions will be presented, and then, we will look at what clues can be uncovered in surveying the actions of God.

August 1519 — Cotignac, Provence — France Apparitions of Our Lady of Graces

On August 10-11, 1519, the Virgin Mary appears on Mount Verdaille, a hill near the village of Cotignac in the South of France, to Jean de la Baume, a logger. She is holding the Child Jesus in Her arms. Beside Her are Saint Michael the Archangel and Saint Bernard. She delivers this message to Jean:

> **"I am the Virgin Mary. Go and tell the clergy and the Consuls of Cotignac to**

build me a church on this place in the name of Our Lady of Graces, and that they should come in procession to receive the gifts which I wish to bestow."[8]

On September 14, 1519, the Feast of the Holy Cross, less than a month after the apparitions, the first stone of the Sanctuary is laid. The entire community comes in procession on Mount Verdaille led by the clergy and officials of the village. Once built, it becomes known as the Shrine of Our Lady of Graces.

One hundred eighteen (**18**) years later, on November 3, 1637, an Augustinian religious, Brother Fiacre, has a vision of the Virgin Mary while praying in Our Lady of Victories Basilica in Paris, France asking him to pray three novenas to Her so that King Louis XIII and Queen Anne, who were childless though married for 22 years, could have a son. In the arms of the Virgin Mary She held a child, which She said *was the future Crown Prince of France*. On the last day of the last novena, exactly nine months later,

Queen Anne gave birth to a son. France finally had an heir to the throne. Moved by these events, King Louis XIII, in February 1638, consecrated himself, his throne and France to the Virgin Mary.

Twenty-three years later, on February 21, 1660, King Louis XIV, heir to his father's throne, journeyed with his mother, Queen Anne, to Cotignac to give thanks for his life at the shrine of Our Lady of Graces.

Apparition of Saint Joseph

Less than four months after the King's visit to Our Lady's shrine, on June 7, 1660, Gaspard Ricard, a young shepherd, is very thirsty on Mount Bessillon, located in the same region as Cotignac. The boy suddenly sees an old man before him who says his name is Joseph. The man says:

> "I am Joseph, lift that rock and you will drink."[9]

The boy protested that it was too heavy to move, but Joseph encouraged him to try, and the boulder moved easily. Upon moving it, a spring burst forth and Gaspard immediately gulped down the fresh cold water. When he turned to thank the man, he had disappeared.

On this very day, returning from Spain with his new wife, Louis XIV, while passing near Our Lady's shrine, hears of the apparition of St. Joseph. He is very moved by the coincidence of the apparition being so close to where Our Lady had appeared that on March 19, 1661, he consecrated his kingdom to St. Joseph just as his father had consecrated the kingdom to the Virgin Mary 23 years before.

Louis XIV, known as Louis the Great or the Sun King, was King of France from May 1643 until his death in 1715. His reign of 72 years and 110 days is the longest recorded of any monarch of a sovereign country in European history.

1873 — Santa Fe, New Mexico

In 1859, Santa Fe, New Mexico's local bishop gave an order for a chapel to be built and named the Chapel of Our Lady of Light. It would be placed under the care of the Sisters of Loretto who would be starting a school for girls. When the chapel was completed, to the dismay of everyone, it was discovered that the builders overlooked the necessity of a staircase to lead up to the choir loft. Experts said the chapel was too small to build a conventional staircase and recommended demolishing the loft. The Sisters, instead, began a novena to St. Joseph for his help in finding a solution.

After the novena ended, a man, unknown to anyone in the region, came with carpentry tools and told the sisters that he could build the staircase, but before he would begin, he insisted on having complete privacy. According to written testimonies and the oral history passed down through generations, the man, whose name was Joseph, locked himself in the chapel. He had with him only a saw, a square and a few other simple tools. He worked for three months until the job was completed. He left as mysteriously as he came, asking for no compensation.

The built staircase is stunning. It was built without nails or glue and has no central support, while it takes two full turns over its axis until it reaches the choir. Experts who have looked at the construction have said that it is impossible that it is standing. Outside of the mysterious builder and the physics of its structure, the wood used to build the staircase is also a mystery as it cannot be identified as to where it came from and how it got there. The Sisters came to only one conclusion—St. Joseph himself built the staircase. The staircase is still intact and preserved. I have been to the Chapel and there is an undeniable sense of the supernatural when you see the staircase and view its construction.

1879 — Knock, Ireland

It was in the evening of August 21, 1879, the vigil of the future date for the Feast of the Queenship of Our Lady, around 8:30 PM. Our Lady appeared with St. Joseph on Her right side, and St. John the Evangelist on Her left. Seeing a bright light coming from the Church, a couple of women went to investigate and were awed at the sight. One ran home to get her family and neighbors. In all, about 15 people of all ages gathered outside, in the pouring rain, before the illuminated figures. Their eyewitness testimony gave exact details of the apparition.

> *"To the left of the altar were the three figures: St. Joseph on the left Our Lady in the middle, and St. John the Evangelist on the right. St. Joseph's hair and beard were gray, and he leaned in a respectful manner toward Mary.*

St. John was dressed in Mass vestments with a bishop's miter on his head, a book in his left hand, and his right hand raised in blessing. Our Lady was life-sized; the other two were smaller.

"The Virgin's eyes were raised toward Heaven with hands outstretched…She wore a white gown and sash. A veil flowed from the back of Her head to Her feet. On top of Her head was a gold crown. Between the crown and the edge of the veil was a gold rose.

"They were about two to three feet out from the Church wall. They said nothing, but as we approached, they seemed to go back a little toward the gable…I was so close I could see the lines and letters inside the book that St. John held. I also saw the wings of the angels fluttering." [10]

The Church officially approved the apparitions in 1936.

1917 — Fatima, Portugal

On May 13, 1917, Our Lady began appearing to three children in Fatima, Portugal, in a field called the Cova da Iria, where they pastured their sheep. She asked the three children whose names were Lucia Santos, and her cousins, Francisco and Jacinta Marto, to meet at this field on the 13th of the next six months. In these apparitions, Our Lady came with warnings for the world if the requests of God were ignored. She offered refuge in Her Immaculate Heart and requested for those who would heed Her voice to make reparation for the sins of the world. She also came with secrets and it was regarding these secrets that Our Lady, in Her apparitions in Medjugorje, said She had come to fulfill.

In the Fatima apparitions, St. Joseph, who had until this time in previous apparitions, taken a more passive role, was now lifted out from the background, into the foreground with Our Lady. In fact, in the September 13, 1917, apparition, Our Lady announced to the visionaries that in Her last apparition of October 13, 1917, St. Joseph would be coming, with the Christ Child, to bless the world. Her words on that September day were:

> **"Continue to say the Rosary to bring about the end of the war** [World War I]. **In October, Our Lord will come also, and Our Lady of Sorrows, and Our Lady of Mount Carmel,** *and Saint Joseph with the Child, to bless the world."*[11]

Torrential rains fell on the day of the final apparition of Fatima, October 13, 1917. The climax of the apparition was what has become known as the Miracle of the Sun. After speaking to the children, Our Lady opened her hands and from them a ray of light emanated in the direction of the sun. The cry of Lucia to look at the sun was heard and spread around to the multitudes gathered. It was the moment when the promised sign was given. The rain that had drenched everyone and made the field a muddy mess suddenly stopped. The sun became, not dazzling, but exceptionally bright. It began to "dance" in the sky and then suddenly, it seemed to be falling from the sky heading to the earth. The crowd was terrorized, fell to their knees and many cried out to God for mercy.

At this moment, the visionaries beheld Our Lady again, dressed in white as bright as the sun with a blue cape, and **St. Joseph holding the Child Jesus stood next to Her, blessing the world**. Then after this vision, they saw the Lord Jesus blessing the world standing next to Our Lady of Sorrows. After these visions, Our Lady of Mount Carmel appeared at the end of the apparition, while at the same time, the miracle ended. The people became aware that their clothes were completely dry. Regarding St. Joseph in this October 13 apparition, Lucia said:

> "We saw, beside the sun, St. Joseph and the Child Jesus and Our Lady. St. Joseph and the Child Jesus appeared to bless the world, for they traced the Sign of the Cross with their hands." [12]

Drawing Conclusions from the Four Apparitions

Clearly a progression can be seen in the way St. Joseph is seen in each apparition, a progression of introduction and of purpose in Joseph's role.

ACT I: Cotignac, Provence – France (1519) —
In this apparition, Our Lady is center stage with Her Son, Jesus. St. Joseph shares the same stage, as his apparition is in the same location,

but he is not on the stage at the same time as Our Lady. Yet, it can't be denied that the "scenes" are connected together in a singular "play," as the area became known as the Village of the "Holy Family." Though separate apparitions, they are seen as singular, connected, each fulfilling their purpose and function.

ACT II: Santa Fe, New Mexico (1873) —

St. Joseph, in this apparition, has a solo act, though Our Lady's presence is felt in the name of the chapel, *"Chapel of Our Lady of Light."* The Sisters of Loretto, who are the caretakers of the chapel, hail from Loretto, Kansas, where German Catholic immigrants settled and where a Catholic priest named the village, "Loretto." It is in Loreto, Italy, where Our Lady's house was said to have been carried by angels from Nazareth, when it was threatened by war, and brought to Italy. This is the same house where the Annunciation took place and the home of the Holy Family after they returned from Egypt. While Our Lady's presence was indirectly a part of this scene, what was in the spotlight was Joseph as a capable worker and provider, Joseph as a very skilled carpenter and artisan, Joseph generous with his time and full of charity in meeting a need without asking for compensation, Joseph the guardian of the consecrated, Joseph as a diligent worker, and Joseph, as father of Jesus, is connected to the power of miracles through grace to accomplish impossible problems.

These specific virtues were formally recognized by the Church, in 1955, when Pope Pius XII granted Joseph a second day to honor him, naming May 1st, the Feast of St. Joseph the Worker. St. Joseph is presented as a model for all Christians to follow in virtue and in offering one's work for the glory of God. At the time, May 1st, a day the Church honors the Virgin Mary, was being taken over by Communists who celebrated it as "International Worker's Day," promoting the rights of man while rejecting God as man's Maker. St. Joseph was being placed on the front lines of this battle that would soon engulf the whole world.

ACT III: Knock, Ireland (1879) — In the apparition at Knock, St. Joseph, with John the Evangelist, finally shares the same stage—same time, same place—with Our Lady. But while Our Lady is seen as "life-size," both Joseph and John are smaller, and standing a little back from Our Lady. There is no speaking by anyone. There is only silence, but the silence speaks loudly as one must study the scene itself and discern the actions of Heaven. In this apparition, though St. Joseph is present, St. John seems to be upstaging Joseph. St. John is dressed in Sacred vestments, arms outstretched dramatically, holding an open book that appears to be the Sacred Scriptures in one hand, while his other hand is raised in a blessing.

Quite the opposite is seen of St. Joseph. His body is somewhat bent in holy reverence, towards

cont'd on pg 50

The miraculous staircase that was allegedly built by St. Joseph in answer to a novena to this saint by the Sisters of Loretto. The architect of their newly built chapel had neglected to allow space for a staircase to the choir loft. The staircase was built sometime between 1877 and 1881, during a century when several other apparitions of St. Joseph were developing a stronger devotion to the most hidden of all saints.

This photograph, taken in 1880, shows hundreds praying at the south gable of the Church of St. John the Baptist, at Knock, County Mayo, Ireland, where an apparition of the Virgin with St. Joseph and St. John was reportedly seen in 1879.

The apparition of Knock, Ireland, in 1879, just as the small group of parishioners saw it. Our Lady, in the middle, stands crowned, with St. John the Evangelist in priestly vestments holding an open book on one side, and Joseph, in humble attire, bowing towards Our Lady on the other. The Lamb of God stands on the altar beside St. John.

In Fatima, Portugal, in the last apparitions to the three young visionaries, St. Joseph appears on October 13, 1917, holding the Child Jesus, with Our Lady beside them. Jesus and Joseph both have their hands raised in a blessing for the world.

In the Bible, a miracle involving an almond branch determines that the Tribe of Levi would be chosen to provide Israel's priests. The Israelites are at a low point. Korah has tried to lead a rebellion against Moses, and God has punished him and his accomplices while sending the plague to finish off the thousands of men who have supported them. In Numbers 17, God instructs Moses to obtain a staff, or branch, from each of the 12 tribal leaders and to put them into the tent of meeting in front of the Ark of the Covenant.

> ***"The man whom I shall choose, his rod shall bud; and I will make to cease from Me the murmurings of the children of Israel, which they murmur against you,"*** the Lord tells Moses in Numbers 17:20.

Moses does as he is told.

> ***"And it came to pass on the morrow, that Moses went into the tent of the testimony; and, behold, the rod of Aaron for the house of Levi was budded, and put forth buds, and bloomed blossoms, and bore ripe almonds,"*** reads the Scripture in the Book of Numbers 17:8.

Why almonds? In nature, the almond flowers first, but takes a long time to produce ripe fruit. Aaron's branch not only budded but blossomed and produced ripe almonds all at the same time — something that any farmer of the period would have known to be impossible, but for a miracle.

Joseph with the Child Jesus and the Flowering Rod, by Alonso Miguel de Tovar. Italian mystic, Maria Valtorta, recorded in her works, The Poem of the Man-God, the scene of Joseph's rod flowering, that led him to become the husband of the Virgin. In the scene, Joseph reveals to the Virgin Mary where he found the rod he brought with him:

> "Look: this is a branch of the almond tree near the house [of the Virgin Mary's parents]. I wanted to pick it … because I thought that if I should be the chosen one, You would have been pleased to have a flower from Your garden…Here is the branch, Mary. With it I offer You my heart, that, like it, has bloomed up till now only for the Lord and is now blooming for You, my spouse.[14]

Did Joseph purposely choose a branch from an almond tree remembering that Aaron's rod was also from an almond tree, or was he led by the Holy Spirit to that tree in Mary's garden? Whatever the truth may be, one can imagine that both Joseph and Mary pondered the miracle on many occasions and how it related to the miracle in Moses' day.

On Our Lady's Feast of the Immaculate Conception, Pope Pius IX decreed St. Joseph, Protector of the Universal Church. On March 19th, he is honored as the Husband of the Blessed Virgin Mary, while on May 1st, a second feast day in his honor, he is remembered as St. Joseph the Worker. This date coincides with the secular International Workers' Day promoted by the labor movement and left-wing parties since the 1890s, and reflects Joseph's status as patron saint of workers.

"*I*nspired by the Gospel, the Fathers of the Church from the earliest centuries stressed that just as St. Joseph took loving care of Mary and gladly dedicated himself to Jesus Christ's upbringing, he likewise watches over and protects Christ's Mystical Body, that is, the Church."

—Pope Saint John Paul II

cont'd from pg 42

his Spouse, the Virgin Mary. While John looks out at the crowd, Joseph's head is bent downward facing Our Lady. Our Lady is dressed in queenly clothes, with a crown on Her head, while Joseph is wearing clothing of a common man, though dignified and as a gentleman. Yet, it cannot be dismissed as unimportant or insignificant that in this Scene of Act III, he is sharing the stage with Our Lady.

What is the meaning of St. John's gesture and attitude? I may not have been able to answer this several years ago, but since traveling to the Island of Patmos, Greece, where John received the visions contained in the book of Revelation, John was present in this apparition, standing at the threshold of time that would begin in Fatima, and be fulfilled through Medjugorje: the time of Revelation. This apparition is deeply prophetic in that it was setting the stage for the Woman of Revelation, in Chapter 12, to make Her grand entrance onto the world stage in the apparitions, first in Fatima, and finally in Medjugorje.

It is the Medjugorje visionaries who say they see Our Lady, standing on a cloud, clothed in the light of the Sun with 12 Stars above Her head—Revelation come to life. Who would Heaven choose for such a moment as this, but John, the only witness of these visions of the end times? The Lamb of God standing on the altar to John's side confirms this as in the Book of Revelation, the imagery of Jesus as the Lamb of God is seen repeatedly.

With such a lofty role given to John, what can be said of St. Joseph's humble demeanor? He is always the humble, hidden witness, the silent adorer of Jesus and servant to his Spouse. Does one think for a minute that either Jesus or Our Lady would be satisfied with the depiction of St. Joseph as a lesser saint than many other popular saints known and loved in the Church today? No, Saint Joseph does not have a subservient position to John in this apparition, rather, the message given in this apparition is that Joseph's time is coming. Joseph is present with Our Lady and with the Lamb of God, not as a secondary figure, but part of the larger picture that will unfold in the coming decades, finding their fulfillment in the apparitions in Medjugorje. It is in the apparitions of Fatima that this can be seen more clearly.

ACT IV: Fatima, Portugal (1917) —

Amazingly, in the apparitions of Fatima, Saint Joseph is not only present on stage with Our Lady, but Our Lady actually announces that he is going to be appearing on stage ahead of time. Why would She do that? She is like an announcer narrating a story that gives everyone a heads up before an important event is about to happen. "Hey, everyone, pay attention to this next act." But in the end, the miracle of the sun got bigger attention than St. Joseph. He faded into the background, like always, compared to the great supernatural event of the "dancing sun." Yet, in reality, it was St. Joseph who was the big story that day, though it went unnoticed and under reported.

Why do I say that? Again, you have to look at where St. Joseph is in relation to Our Lady on the stage. He is sharing the stage, for the first time, alone with Our Lady. He isn't smaller than Her. They both are life-sized. And it is Joseph who is holding the Christ Child in his arms. Both Joseph and Jesus have their hands raised and are blessing the world. Wait? Joseph is blessing the world? How does he do that? Who gives him the authority to bless? Our Lady blesses, but She is the Queen of Heaven. What position does Joseph hold? Remember when Jesus' authority was being questioned while He walked the earth? What did people say of Jesus?

> ***They said, "Is this not Jesus, the son of Joseph, whose father and mother we know? How can he now say, 'I came down from heaven'?"*** John 6:42

Are we missing something in this apparition? What is Our Lady doing while Joseph and Jesus are blessing the world? She is normally the one in center stage. But, at this moment in the apparition, She is silently standing next to Joseph, as he blesses the world with Jesus, their Son. Does this not give us a better understanding of who St. Joseph is? The Fatima visionaries then see the scene fade and another take its place. Now, a grown Jesus is there with His Mother by His side. St. Joseph is no longer on the stage.

When one speaks about the Fatima apparitions, Joseph gets mentioned, but only as a minor actor. Why is that? Why has God allowed Joseph to remain in obscurity? Because Joseph has been saved for such a time as this. When Our Lady foretold Joseph's appearance in the last apparition of Fatima, was She foretelling a greater entrance of Joseph on the world's stage before the end of Her apparitions in Medjugorje? The clues being gathered suggest that She is.

A Few Other Thoughts Concerning the Symbolism in the Apparitions

The Spring

In the June 7, 1660, apparition, in Contignac, France, Joseph points out a **hidden spring** to a thirsty boy, who quenches his thirst in the stream. What does the spring represent? We know, for one, a spring represents the Divine Mercy of God. Our Lady speaks of this Herself in Her messages in Medjugorje.

October 2, 2014

> "…You, my children… are thirsty. You thirst for peace, love and happiness. Drink out of my hands. My hands are offering to you my Son who is the spring of clear water…."

October 2, 2019

> "...You, my children—you who always thirst for more love, truth, and faith—need to know that there is only one spring from which you can drink. It is trust in the Heavenly Father; it is trust in His love..."

There have been other times Our Lady has mentioned the word "spring" in Her messages. We also know that Our Lady pointed out **a hidden spring** to Bernadette Soubirous, in the grotto of Lourdes, France, in 1858, in Her apparitions there. Will we see a hidden spring appear in Medjugorje as part of the Secrets that will bring the apparitions full circle? Our Lady, on another occasion, mentions spring in Her message:

April 2, 2014

> "...All those who do not know my Son, all those thirsting for the love and

peace of my Son, will drink from this spring..."

Turn to the Book of Revelation and you will also read about a spring:

> *"For the Lamb who is in the center of the throne will shepherd them and lead them to springs of life-giving water."*
> Revelation 7:17

Or here, at the beginning of the last chapter in Revelation, which speaks also of Our Lady messages:

> *"Then the angel showed me the river of life-giving water, sparkling like crystal, flowing from the throne of God and of the Lamb down the middle of its street. One either side of the river grew the tree of life that produces fruit twelve times a year, once each month; the leaves of the trees serve as medicine for the nations."*
> Revelation 22:1–2

It is the spring that feeds the Tree of Life, that is producing fruit twelve times a year, once each month (Our Lady's monthly messages to Marija). The leaves of the trees, the messages, are medicine for the nations. The mercy of God, the life-giving water that Scripture speaks of, comes in many forms to us. Our Lady, Herself, is the greatest mercy of God for our time. Will St. Joseph prove also to be a great gift of mercy for our time?

The Staircase

In the story of the miracle staircase in Sante Fe, New Mexico, there was no access to the choir loft due to the lack of stairs to get there (see picture on page 43). Today, there are too many souls who have no access to Heaven because they have lost the means of getting there. St. Joseph provided the bridge, or the steps to get to the choir loft. Is God preparing to use St. Joseph with Our Lady and Jesus, the Holy Trinity known as the Holy Family, to rebuild the steps to the Kingdom, particularly in the family, so souls will have access to Heaven again?

But, there also may be another symbol for the staircase. Consider this quote from Blessed William Joseph Chaminade:

"Picture to yourself the sanctity of all the patriarchs of old, that long line of successive generations **which is the mysterious ladder of Jacob**, *culminating in the person of the Son of God. See how great was the faith of Abraham, the obedience of Isaac, the courage of David, the wisdom of Solomon. After you have formed the highest opinion of these saints, remember that Joseph is at the top of the ladder, at the head of the saints, the kings, the prophets, the patriarchs, that he is more faithful than Abraham, more obedient than Isaac, more generous than David, wiser than Solomon, in a word, as superior in grace as he is close to the source, Jesus sleeping in his arms."* [13]

Is Joseph the Patriarch at the top of the staircase? Joseph is superior in grace than all other saints because he is closest to the Source. As the earthly father of Jesus, Joseph knows how to lead hearts to Christ like no one else, having been taught by both Jesus and Our Lady. And he has been waiting for two millenniums to finally join them on the world's stage.

Jesus, speaking of St. Joseph before entering into Passion Week:

"Be just. Just like him who was My guardian for so many years...Holy servant of God!...A new Abraham, with a broken heart, but with perfect will, he would not have advised Me to be cowardly." [15]

<u>The Poem of the Man-God</u>
Volume V, p.154-155

CHAPTER FIVE

A Mystery of St. Joseph Revealed

Why is there so much mystery surrounding St. Joseph. Was Joseph just randomly selected by God to fill a vacant position? Common sense tells us that God would not leave anything regarding the coming of the Messiah to random choice. Our Lady said:

February 2, 2019

> **"…you are not united by chance. The Heavenly Father does not unite anyone by chance…"**

This would be especially true for the two who would become the parents of Jesus on earth. Jesus, in order to be accepted as the true Messiah, had to fulfill certain requirements mandated through the prophetic words of prophets throughout thousands of millennia.

One of the first litmus tests of anyone claiming to be the Messiah was that he had to come from the lineage of King David. The Book of Matthew starts off with a genealogy of Jesus Christ, showing his lineage starting from Adam, through King David, that finally led to Joseph.

> *"Eleazar became the father of Matthan, Matthan the father of Jacob, Jacob the father of Joseph, the husband of Mary. Of her was born Jesus who is called the Messiah.*
>
> *"Thus, the total number of generations from Abraham to David is fourteen generations; from David to the Babylonian exile, fourteen generations; from the Babylonian exile to*

the Messiah, fourteen generations."
Matthew 1:14–17

What is the purpose of the genealogy? It is to show that Joseph, son of Jacob came from the royal lineage of David, giving legitimacy to Jesus' claim to Messiah, the Promised Deliverer of God's people. In showing this, what does this say concerning Joseph? **Was the poor carpenter from Nazareth the rightful heir to the throne?**

At the end of the genealogy, it says there were 14 generations from Adam until King David and then 14 generations from King David to the Babylonian exile. The Babylonian exile effectively ended the Kingdom of Israel. Without a kingdom to rule, there was no longer a need for a king. While the bloodlines of David's sons continued to be traced through the generations, there was no kingdom to inherit, no power, no authority. Yet, it still mattered from Heaven's viewpoint. If Jesus was to be the Messiah, the Savior of His people, His earthly authority had to come through the lineage of David. Joseph's lineage reaches back to King Solomon, who was son and successor of David. If the Kingdom of Israel had not been dismantled all those generations ago, would **Joseph have risen to the throne of Israel as its king?**

Church tradition says that when it was time to choose a husband for the Virgin Mary, all the eligible men in the line of David were requested to come to Jerusalem, each with a barren tree branch. The High Priest asked God for a sign to show forth His will regarding the Virgin's husband. Of all the barren branches clustered together, it was Joseph's branch, and only his branch, that miraculously burst out in fresh flowery blooms; an undeniable sign of God's choice.

When you see a picture or statue of St. Joseph, he is often depicted holding a stem of lilies, almost as if he was holding a scepter. What is a scepter? An ornamental staff held by kings as a symbol of their authority and sovereignty. It actually carries a higher importance as a sign of the king's authority than the crown itself.

Is there an Old Testament story involving a staff that miraculously bloomed? Not only is the answer "yes," but the alignment of that story with what happened with Joseph is so evident that it becomes obvious the two events are connected. In the days of Moses, when the Israelites were tempted to overthrow Moses and Aaron with other leaders, God intervened and through Moses, demanded each of the Tribes of Israel to bring forth a barren branch to set in the Tabernacle, or Tent of Meeting, overnight. When everyone returned the next morning, Aaron's rod had miraculously flowered, giving a physical manifestation that God's authority rested upon Aaron which gave warning to the Israelites not to reject the leader whom God had chosen for them.

Even before Moses' time, the rod or staff was the material object God gave to the Patriarchs to show His sovereignty. God anointed Moses' rod to manifest the plagues upon Egypt to prove He was the One True God, more powerful than any of their gods. Through the grace of God, Moses used the same rod to part the Red Sea in deliverance of God's people, and to bring forth fresh water from a rock in the desert for the same reason. When the rod was raised up in battle, Israel was victorious over their enemy. When the rod was passed down from Moses to Joshua, Joshua led the Israelites into the Promised Land with the rod in hand. David held the staff when he fought and killed Goliath. All the kings after him had a staff as their scepter. Many Biblical scholars believe that it was the same miraculous staff that was handed down generation after generation.

There is one particular detail of the story of Aaron's rod not yet revealed that ties it to Joseph's rod. The Tabernacle in the wilderness held within it the Ark of the Covenant. All the barren branches of the Tribes of Israel were placed before the Ark and left there until the action of God bloomed forth Aaron's branch. The Ark of the Covenant would eventually become the "Tabernacle" that housed the 10 Commandments (Law of God), Aaron's staff and a remnant of the manna, the bread from Heaven, that fed the Israelites in the desert. When, centuries later, Israel was defeated by the Babylonian Empire, the Ark of the Covenant mysteriously disappeared, never to be found. As the geneology testifies—14 generations from King David to the Babylonian exile, and then 14 generations from the exile to the coming of the Messiah. What then do we find?

Joseph, along with all the men of the lineage of David gathered their barren branches and placed them where? Just as Aaron did, before the Ark of the Covenant. But Joseph placed his branch before the "New" Ark, the Virgin Mary, who would become the Tabernacle for the Word of God in Flesh (the Law of God) and the Bread from Heaven (the Manna/Eucharist). Joseph's branch flowering (Aaron's rod) was the indisputable sign that he was not only chosen, but was being given God's full authority and power in fulfilling his role as guardian and protector of the Ark (Our Lady) and Who would come to dwell within Her (Jesus). Aaron was from the Tribe of Levi. What particular role did God assign the Levites and Aaron in particular? They were the protectors of the Tabernacle and the Ark and were ordained, particularly, for the service of God. If this is true of Aaron, how much more so is it true for Joseph, who was charged with the responsibility of caring and protecting Our Lady, the New Ark, and the Word made Flesh Who would become the Bread of Life?

God made the miracle happen for Joseph. Doesn't that suggest that Joseph would have been the successor to the throne if Israel had remained a nation? Jesus, being Joseph's Son, could then rightfully take the throne of Israel and be named King legally. But, actually, no. There was one obstacle that would have prevented Jesus from mounting the throne through Joseph's lineage. It has to do with a curse that God placed upon one of the kings of Israel by the name of Jeconiah, the last king before the Babylonian exile. He so angered God that judgment came upon him and he was forcefully taken from the throne and sent into exile, never to return to his fatherland again. But God placed a further indictment against him:

> ***"No descendant of his shall achieve a seat on the throne of David as ruler again over Judah."*** Jeremiah 22:30

Because of this curse, Joseph, even though a descendant of David, could never mount the throne of Israel. Then how could Jesus have the legal right to claim He is the Messiah? Amazingly, it comes not through Joseph's lineage, but through Mary's. In fact, that is what Matthew's genealogy is pointing to when he wrote:

"Jacob the father of Joseph, **the husband of Mary.** <u>*Of Her*</u> *was born Jesus who is called the Messiah."* Matthew 1:16

In the Book of Luke, the genealogy of Mary's lineage is given. Whereas, Joseph came through David's son, Solomon, Mary's lineage came through David's son, Nathan. There was no curse on Nathan's lineage. Therefore, Jesus' Kingship came through Mary. So, then was there no significance to Joseph's selection after all? Again, as Our Lady said:

September 2, 2016

"…nothing is by chance…"

In Hebrew Law, when a man marries a woman, everything the woman owns becomes her husbands. So, Mary's Son, Jesus, legally becomes Joseph's son, and Jesus, though He does not share in the bloodline of Joseph, inherits from Joseph, the royal title of Joseph's kingship. Even though Jesus became Joseph's son by means of adoption, Joseph could pass on the fullness of his kingship to Jesus after he died because Jesus was Joseph's son fully and legally in the eyes of the Hebrew Law. And isn't it prophetic that, according to Church tradition, Joseph died just before Jesus began His public ministry.

Jesus is tied then to both bloodlines of royalty, but it is Mary's that gives Him the right to claim the title of Messiah. Yet, even so, both Mary and Jesus honored and submitted to Joseph as the head of their house. In <u>The Poem of the Man God</u>, Jesus speaks of Joseph and how esteemed he was in their little home:

> *"Joseph was the head of the family, and as such, his authority was undisputed and indisputable: Before it the Spouse and Mother of God bent reverently and the Son of God submitted Himself willingly. Whatever Joseph decided to do, was well done: There were no*

discussions…no oppositions. His word was our little law."[16]

There is further significance to Joseph being God's choice to be the earthly father of His Son. But to understand it more deeply, we have to take a closer look into the mystery. And it is Our Lady's desire that we:

September 25, 2017

> **"…may witness Heaven and Heavenly mysteries…"**

"Our Lady of Medjugorje first appeared on the Feast of John the Baptist, June 24, 1981. Who was John the Baptist? According to Jesus in Scripture, the greatest prophet who ever lived and the announcer of the coming of the Messiah. What is the purpose of Our Lady's apparitions in Medjugorje? Among others, it is to prepare the world for the Second Coming of Her Son, Jesus Christ."

Friend of Medjugorje

CHAPTER SIX

John the Baptist: The Last Priest

J ohn the Baptist, like Joseph, had a specific purpose in Salvation history. Isaiah had prophesied his coming:

> *"A voice cries out in the wilderness, prepare the way for the LORD; and in the desert a straight highway for our God."* Isaiah 40:3

Why was John chosen out of all men of the time? A Protestant pastor gives a plausible answer to that question in his writing: *"John the Baptist: The Last Priest."* Pastor Randy White makes the case that John the Baptist was *the only one who could be chosen because of who he was.* Jesus said in Mark 2:27,

"The Sabbath was made for man, not man for the Sabbath." In the same way:

"The prophecy of the Old Testament did not create the need for John but foretold the man who was John." [17]

Who was John's father? He is introduced in Luke 1:5 when it is stated, **"...there was a Priest."** Why is that significant? John was chosen to be the forerunner of Christ. It was he who was to herald the coming of the Messiah as messenger and mediator between God and His people. This "job description" is found often in the Old Testament and is assigned only to a "priest" or a "prophet". Sometimes a singular man held both titles. We know that John was considered a prophet, but is there evidence that he was also a priest?

John's father, Zechariah, was a Levite, meaning he was a priest specifically chosen to serve in the Temple. Also, of great importance, both Zechariah and his wife, Elizabeth, were descendants of Aaron, the first priest of Israel. This makes John, from both sides of his bloodline, a descendent from the priestly stock of Aaron.

Zechariah and Elizabeth were childless and were advanced in age. Having prayed for so many years for a child, they refused to give up hope that God may still answer their prayer. On the day that Zechariah went to the Temple to offer this intention to the Lord, "by lot," or in other words, by the hand of the Holy Spirit, he was chosen out of a multitude of priests, to be the one to enter the Sanctuary to burn incense for the whole assembly. It is at this moment, when he is in the Holy of Holies that God reveals to him that Elizabeth is to bear a child and his name will be John. Pastor White explains the significance of this:

> *"Zechariah was chosen by the invisible hand of God on that particular day because, it seems, God wanted a particular man to work*

in the Temple and do the work of the High Priest. Is Luke revealing to us that God is rejecting the man that the Caesar had chosen as High Priest [a political appointment rather than a spiritual appointment], and He, God, himself, is choosing Zechariah, a man without a child, fulfilling—even if for a day—his rightful role as High Priest? If so, this would mean we have come to the end of the line in the Aaronic Priesthood, unless Zechariah has a son." [18]

We know the story and what was said of John:

> **"He will be great in the sight of the Lord. And he will drink no wine or liquor. And he will be filled with the Holy Spirit, while yet in his mother's womb, and he will turn many of the sons of Israel back to the Lord God. It is he who will go as a forerunner before him."** Luke 1:15

Is that not what a Priest is called to be? Is this not the duty and responsibility of a priest of God? So, to put it in the right perspective, White writes:

> *"It appears that God has decided that what appeared to be the end of the line would not be the end of the line, after all. God was going to give a son to Zechariah and Elizabeth,* **and he would be the last of the High Priests of the order of Aaron."** [19]

Following this progression, Pastor White leads to a conclusion, even a revelation, concerning the Baptist. He states:

> *"In Malachi 3:1 God tells us that he will send a 'messenger' to prepare the way of the Lord. In the context of Malachi, the messenger is always a Priest. God, through Malachi, is speaking to a group of Priests with whom he is sorely dissatisfied. God promises to these messengers that he is going to send, 'my mes-*

senger' who will be a 'messenger of the covenant.' Is God saying that since the Priests of the order of Aaron are not doing their work, he is going to send his own Priest? That is, a Priest after the order of Melchizedek? And, when John the Baptist arrives, what does he do? He is most known for baptizing. And when Jesus wanted to be baptized, John, at first, refused. He refused on the basis of his unworthiness, that he was baptizing a baptism of repentance, and Jesus had nothing of which he needed to repent. Jesus, however, said 'for righteousness, let it be done.' What righteousness is he talking about?

"When Aaron was ordained to be the Priest, the ordination service included the 'washing' of Aaron, and his sons. The particular Hebrew word for wash that is used in the ordination of the Priest is not a word for rinse, or for sprinkling, or for pouring, but it's a word *that means to get all the way into the water. In Judaism, the Mikva* served as the baptistery. A Jew would go into the Mikva and be completely submerged into the water. When the law says that the Priest was to be washed when he was ordained, it is likely referring to a Mikva experience; that is, a baptism by immersion. And when Jesus was ready to begin his ministry, he said, 'Let it be, this is for righteousness sake.' I believe that John, the last of the High Priest, according to the order of Aaron, is baptizing Jesus, the High Priest according to the order of Melchizedek! In other words,* **John is transferring authority to the new order of the Priesthood; the old order of Aaron is passing away, and now is transferred to Jesus**, *who is our Priest according to the Priestly order of Melchizedek.*

---

* In Judaism, the Mikva is a pool of water used for ceremonial cleansing.

> "*If this is true, then who besides John could have been chosen for this task?* **John had to be chosen, because he was the end of the line for the Aaronic Priesthood legitimately passing authority to the new Priesthood, forever held in Jesus Christ!*"* [20]

John was not randomly chosen, but was in the mind of God from the moment God created the earth, and chose the actors for the greatest performance in all of history. But now, let's look back at Joseph.

""It is true that the other saints enjoy great power in heaven, but they ask as servants, and do not command as masters. Saint Joseph, to whose authority Jesus was subject on earth, obtains what he desires from his kingly foster Son in heaven."

St. Thomas Aquinas

CHAPTER SEVEN

St. Joseph: The Last King

Recall that Joseph's bloodline could not produce an heir to the throne. As previously asked, what then is the relevance for Joseph being chosen at all? Pastor White concludes the following:

> *"So, if a son of Joseph cannot be heir to the throne, why was Joseph selected? It is the same reason God chose John the Baptist, because he is the last in the line. John the Baptist is the one that anoints or transfers the authority to the new priestly order, and Joseph is presented as the one that would have had the crown. Joseph takes the crown and, by his adoption of Jesus, he passes the crown to a new line, a line which is not within the pro-*

phetic curse that says that no son of Coniah will ever sit on the throne. Joseph gives the throne while John gives the priestly role and now we have our Priest and our King who had been anointed by the proper authority. Jesus did not highjack the priesthood from the line of Aaron, nor did he highjack the kingdom from the line of Jeconiah. **On both cases the role was given to Him, by the last Priest and the last King."** [21]

The very fact that God chose St. Joseph for Mary's husband and Jesus' foster father leads to the logical conclusion that the "man," Joseph, had within his lineage, his stock, a signifcance necessary to fulfill the prophesies for the coming of the Messiah. Yet, it was not his blood lineage that made him the greatest of all saints. The first king of Israel was Saul. Though he was given the honor of "first," he failed through the sin of pride. Scripture states that the greatest of all of Israel's kings was King David, a man after God's own heart, yet he fell through infidelity which brought scandal and curses upon him, his family and his kingdom. But faihtful Joseph spent his life in humble service to the King of Peace and His Queen Mother without seeking anything for himself. A true servant king. Who can doubt that God will make known the witness of Joseph's life? Who better to do this than the Virgin Mary, Joseph's spouse, who loved him uniquely and was deeply indebted to him for his care of Jesus and Herself? Consider also that if St. Joseph was truly the Last King of Israel, he had to die before Jesus began His mission, whereby he could pass the crown to the long awaited Messiah.

Mary was assumed into Heaven and shortly after, was crowned Queen of Heaven and earth. What about Joseph? While the world is still waiting to know Joseph more intimately, has he already received his throne in Heaven? St. Gertrude the Great, while in ecstasy, beheld Heaven open and saw **St. Joseph seated on a throne. It impressed her to see that every time his name was pronounced, the saints reverently bent their heads in deep respect.** St. Lawrence, a devoted follower of St. Joseph, states:

> *"In any kingdom not only the king and queen, who shine forth in the kingdom like the sun and the moon, but also the kingdom's princes, dukes, governors, etc., and especially the parents and blood relatives of the king, who shine like the stars in the sky, are held in honor by the king's good and faithful subjects. So, my friends, reason certainly demands that in the kingdom of Christ not only Christ and the Blessed Virgin be worthy of high esteem, but also all the saints and especially this blessed man, Joseph, the father of Christ and spouse of the most holy Virgin, be held in highest honor by Christ himself as his father and by the most holy Virgin as her husband."* [22]

St. Lawrence also added:

> *"If Christ sits at the right hand of his Father in the glory of paradise above all the choirs of angels, because He is the first of all the predestined and was the holiest of the holiest in this world, and if the Blessed Virgin, by reason of Her own holiness, holds the second place after Christ because She is also second by reason of predestination from eternity and grace in time, it seems to me that because Joseph holds the third place after Christ in eternal predestination and grace in time, so by the same reasoning he also holds the third place in the glory of paradise."* [23]

Joseph will not be raised, exalted and honored only to be one saint among the many saints. Rather, he will be recognized as the greatest of all saints, second only to Our Lady, within the Holy Trinity of the Family that he was predestined to be a part of on earth. Many speak of the devotion of the Two Hearts, the Two Hearts of Jesus and Mary. But another set of two hearts will rise to be honored and revered, the two hearts of Mary and Joseph, a witness of holy marriage that the world is such in need of today. Through Vicka's diary, is the veil about to be lifted revealing the difficulties and trials they experienced in their life together as they raised the Son of God, yet despite them all, they were able to live a heaven on earth?

> *"Symbolically, in this marriage and family union of Joseph with Mary there was an image of the sacred Trinity. For Joseph represented the Eternal Father, the Blessed Virgin the Holy Spirit, both because She was the most holy, and because She had conceived by the Holy Spirit. Christ represented Himself, even the Son of God. Hence, as there is in the sacred Trinity essentially one God in three Persons, so here was there one marriage and one perfect family, consisting of three per-*

sons, namely, Joseph, Mary, and Christ… This family was then, as it were, a heaven upon earth…" [24]

St. Joseph has been predestined to help to restore not only the family, but also the Church, and those consecrated to God. We look forward, with great anticipation, to the release of Vicka's book on Our Lady's life and what will be revealed about Her and St. Joseph. The mother of the apostles James and John, once pressed Jesus to give her sons preferential seating, to be seated at Jesus' right and left side in Heaven, when He is on His throne. Jesus replied:

> **"'You don't know what you are asking,'" Jesus said to them. 'Can you drink the cup I am going to drink?' 'We can,' they answered. Jesus said to them, 'You will indeed drink from my cup, but to sit at my right or left is not for me to grant. These places belong to**

those for whom they have been prepared by my Father.'" Matthew 20:21–23

It is traditionally held that it is Our Lady, the Mother of Jesus, the Queen Mother, who has the honor of sitting at the right side of Jesus' throne in Heaven. Psalm 45:9 says, *"The queen stands at your right hand, arrayed in gold."* In biblical times, the Queen Mother held a priveledged position of authority with the King and was often the mediator between the King and his subjects. Her position was elevated even above the King's wife. The first mention of a Queen Mother in the Kingdom of Israel was in 1 Kings, referring to Bathsheba, wife of King David and Mother of Solomon, Solomon being the son who succeeded David on the throne.

When Solomon's mother, Bathsheba, entered his palace one day, Solomon *"rose to meet her and bowed down to her. Then he sat on his throne and had a seat brought for the king's mother, and she sat on his right."* 1 Kings 2:19 The King of Israel had given his Mother a seat at his right hand, the privileged position of authority. This was a foreshadowing of the Virgin Mary who would become the Queen Mother of the Son of God. This is why it is believed that Our Lady sits at Christ's right hand in Heaven. But who is it that sits at His left side? Will we be surprised if it is Joseph, Jesus' earthly father, the Last King of Israel?

> *Eternal Father, by Thy love for St. Joseph, whom Thou didst select from among all men to represent Thee upon earth, have mercy on us and on the dying. Amen.*

"He is Holy Joseph, because according to the opinion of a great number of doctors, he, as well as St. John Baptist, was sanctified even before he was born. He is Holy Joseph, because his office, of being spouse and protector of Mary, specially demanded sanctity. He is Holy Joseph, because no other saint but he lived in such and so long intimacy and familiarity with the source of all holiness, Jesus, God incarnate, and Mary, the holiest of Creatures."

St. John Henry Newman

APPENDIX

Paralleling Heaven's Actions, the Popes Follow Suit

Giving Saint Joseph nothing more than an occasional nod of the head for 1,800 years, suddenly the popes of the past two centuries began taking St. Joseph out of the shadows and into the light, following the lead of the faithful whose devotion to St. Joseph was steadily growing. It shouldn't be surprising that many of the actions of the popes ended up aligning to the period of time of the apparitions—Heaven moves and then the Church moves from the prayers of the faithful that come from the response of the people to the actions of Heaven.

1621— The primary feast of St. Joseph, March 19, was established by Pope Gregory XV.

1870 — St. Joseph is declared the *"Patron of the Universal Church"* by Blessed Pope Pius IX.

1889 — Pope Leo XIII writes *Quamquam Pluries,* an encyclical letter on St. Joseph.

1909 — Pope Saint Pius X officially approves the *Litany of St. Joseph.* The date this happened was on **March 18, 1909**.

1921 — The phrase *"Blessed be St. Joseph, her most chaste spouse"* is inserted into the Divine Praises by Pope Benedict XV.

1955 — *The Feast of St. Joseph the Worker* is established and to be celebrated on May 1, 1955, by Venerable Pope Pius XII.

1962 — St. Joseph's name is inserted into the Canon of the Mass (Eucharistic Prayer I) by Pope Saint John XXIII.

1989 — Pope Saint John Paul II writes *Redemptoris Custos,* an apostolic exhortation on St. Joseph.

2013 — The name of St. Joseph is inserted into all Eucharistic Prayers of the Mass by Pope

Francis. Pope Emeritus Benedict XVI had the intention of doing so but was unable to fulfill this desire when he resigned from his position. Pope Francis followed through with Benedict's intention.

2013 — Vatican City State is consecrated to St. Joseph by Pope Francis.

2021 — In celebration of the 150th anniversary of Blessed Pope Pius IX's declaration of St. Joseph as Patron of the Universal Church, Pope Francis proclaimed a special "Year of St. Joseph," December 8, 2020, to December 8, 2021. It is the first time in Church history where St. Joseph has been given a year dedicated to him.

One word concerning the official approval of the Litany of St. Joseph by Pope Pius X. Litanies are unique prayers in that they define and give "titles" of the virtues of a saint. For St. Joseph's litany to be approved and instituted **on March 18th, rather than March 19th, is a significant sign.**

Endnotes

1. "Joseph's Advice to Jesus" by a Friend of Medjugorje, Caritas of Birmingham, 2019
2. "The Divine Design of the Hebrew Language" https://www.biblewheel.com/Book/Chapters/Chapt07.php
3. https://maryourhelp.org/e-books/st-joseph/Saint-Joseph-the-just-man-and-protector.pdf
4. Ibid.
5. https://aleteia.org/2017/05/19/exclusive-cardinal-caffarra-what-sr-lucia-wrote-to-me-is-being-fulfilled-today/
6. https://www.bravestthing.com/2021/03/a-16th-century-prophecy-about-st-joseph.html
7. "Father, Revelations," by A Friend of Medjugorje, February 5, 2019; https://medjugorje.com/father-revelations/
8. https://www.marypages.com/cotignac-(our-lady-of-grace)-en.html
9. https://blessedjoseph.blogspot.com/2013/08/st-joseph-apparition-cotignac-france.html
10. https://www.homeofthemother.org/en/magazine/selected-articles/spiritual-life/9973-the-history-of-the-apparition-of-our-lady-of-knock
11. Documents on Fatima and the Memoirs of Sister Lucia, Fr. Antonio Maria Martins, S.J., 2002
12. Ibid.
13. https://www.facebook.com/SocComAlaminos/posts/1758723327620629
14. Maria Valtorta, The Poem of the Man-God, Volume 1, pg. 65
15. Maria Valtorta, The Poem of the Man God, Volume V, p. 154–155
16. Maria Valtorta, The Poem of the Man God, Volume I, p. 196
17. https://www.tovrose.com/2014/04/12/john-the-baptist-the-last-priest/
18. Ibid.
19. Ibid.
20. Ibid.
21. https://www.tovrose.com/2014/04/12/john-the-baptist-the-last-priest/
22. https://capuchins.org/wp-content/uploads/2021/03/FIRST-SERMON.pdf
23. Ibid.
24. Ibid.

The Story of Medjugorje

Between Heaven and Earth, written by A Friend of Medjugorje, is a powerful introduction to the story of Medjugorje. Whether one is a believer or not, he will find *Between Heaven and Earth* a moving, powerful introduction and yet an objective way to gently introduce others to Our Lady and Her plans. This, accompanied with the *Reader's Digest* supplement, "A Village Sees the Light," which is also available from Caritas of Birmingham, is a perfect way to introduce Medjugorje.

The Marriage Manual

SAVED TENS OF THOUSANDS OF MARRIAGES AROUND THE WORLD

How to Change Your Husband
Owner's Manual for the Family
By a Friend of Medjugorje

★ Save & Renew Marriage
★ Marriage Preparation
★ Sermons for Priests

See order form in the back of the book to order this book.

All that needs to be said is, just read it.

A Blessing from Heaven, to be used as a tool for conversion. Find out what a Friend of Medjugorje has learned and discerned about this powerful blessing in this short book.

The Economic Time Bomb is Ticking...

Are You Ready?

A Friend of Medjugorje tells you how to be ready for what is coming down soon.

"My son-in-law says: 'people do know how bad things are, but they don't know what to do.' This book tells you <u>what to do right now</u>…"

Jean
Viola, Arkansas

"Being of a different denomination, this book has opened my eyes to see a large conversion of souls in the very near future."

Brett
Birmingham, Alabama

Order Form

Item	Description	Pricing	$
	Medjugorje and the Mysteries of Saint Joseph Soft Cover Books BF130	*Please add shipping and handling.* ☐ 1=FREE please add S&H ☐ 50=$45.00 (90¢ EA) ☐ 10=$12.50 ($1.25 EA) ☐ 100=$80.00 (80¢ EA) ☐ 25=$25.00 ($1.00 EA) ☐ 1,000=$650.00 (65¢ EA)	$
	How to Change Your Husband Soft Cover BF103	*Please add shipping and handling* ☐ 1=$6.00 ☐ 10=$40.00 ($4.00 EA) (For larger quantities call for discounted case pricing.)	$
	"A Blessing to Help Save the World" Short Books BK1019	*Suggested Donation (Please add shipping and handling)* ☐ 1=FREE please add S&H ☐ 50=$17.50 (35¢ EA) ☐ 10=$5.00 (50¢ EA) ☐ 100=$30.00 (30¢ EA) ☐ 25=$10.00 (40¢ EA) ☐ 1,000=$250.00 (25¢ EA)	$
	It Ain't Gonna Happen A Return to Truth Soft Cover Books BF108	*(Please add shipping and handling)* ☐ 1=$15.00 ☐ 10=$70 ($7.00 EA) (For larger quantities call for discounted case pricing.)	$
	Between Heaven and Earth 1 audio CD (60 min.) CD1001	*Please add shipping and handling* ☐ 1=5.00 ☐ 50=$50.00 ($1.00 EA) ☐ 10=$15.00 ($1.50 EA) ☐ 100=$75.00 (75¢ EA) ☐ 20=$25.00 ($1.25 EA) ☐ 1,000=$750.00 (75¢ EA)	$
	"Modesty" Short Books BK1014	*Suggested Donation (Please add shipping and handling)* ☐ 1=FREE please add S&H ☐ 50=$45.00 (90¢ EA) ☐ 10=$12.50 ($1.25 EA) ☐ 100=$80.00 (80¢ EA) ☐ 25=$25.00 ($1.00 EA) ☐ 1,000=$600.00 (60¢ EA)	$
	"They Know, But They Don't Want You to Know. Tired of Hearing About Corona? There's Something You Need to Know." Short Books BK1314	*Suggested Donation (Please add shipping and handling)* ☐ 1=FREE please add S&H ☐ 50=$17.50 (35¢ EA) ☐ 10=$5.00 (50¢ EA) ☐ 100=$30.00 (30¢ EA) ☐ 25=$10.00 (40¢ EA) ☐ 1,000=$300.00 (30¢ EA)	$

Subtotal $

Shipping & Handling

Order Sub-total	UPS SurePost (Standard)	UPS Ground
$0-$10.00	$8.00	$15.00
$10.01-$20.00	$10.50	$17.50
$20.01-$50.00	$13.00	$20.00
$50.01-$100.00	$20.00	$27.00
Over $100.00	20% of total	25% of total

For overnight delivery, call for pricing.
International (Surface): Double above shipping Cost. Call for faster International delivery.

$

TOTAL: $

☎ Ph: (Outside USA add 001) 205-672-2000 ext. 315 USA 24 hrs.
Fax: 205-672-9667 USA 24 hrs.
Mail: **Caritas of Birmingham** 100 Our Lady Queen of Peace Drive Sterrett, AL 35147-9987 USA

Enclose in remittance envelope or call in your order and donation. If you have any questions you may call 205-672-2000 and leave a message on ext. 315. Or call during office hours 8:30 a.m.–5:00 p.m. Central Time Monday–Friday and talk with a real person ☺
The Federal Tax Exempt I.D. # for Caritas of Birmingham is 63-0945243.

Ship to: Name(s) (please print) _____ Birthday: _____
Address _____
City _____ State _____ Zip Code _____
Phone # _____ (if an international number, include all digits)
☐ Payment Enclosed
Credit Card type (check one) ☐ VISA ☐ MasterCard ☐ Discover
Credit Card Number ☐☐☐☐ ☐☐☐☐ ☐☐☐☐ ☐☐☐☐   3-Digit Code on Back: ☐☐☐
Expiration date: ☐☐-☐☐ e-mail: _____